MESSED UP
and Don't Even Know It

The Journey from Childhood Trauma to Healing

MESSED UP
and Don't Even Know It

The Journey from Childhood Trauma to Healing

IRA L. LAKE PhD(c), M.Div, M.A.

Messed Up and Don't Even Know It:
The Journey from Childhood Trauma to Healing
Copyright © 2015 Ira L. Lake PhD(c), M.Div, M.A.

All rights reserved. No part of this book may be reproduced (except for inclusion in reviews), disseminated or utilized in any form or by any means, electronic or mechanical, including photocopying, recording, or in any information storage and retrieval system, or the Internet/World Wide Web without written permission from the author or publisher.

Book design by:
Arbor Books, Inc.
www.arborbooks.com

Printed in the United States of America

Messed Up and Don't Even Know It:
The Journey from Childhood Trauma to Healing
Ira L. Lake PhD(c), M.Div, M.A.

1. Title   2. Author   3. Psychology

Library of Congress Control Number: 2015940042
ISBN 13: 978-0-692-43991-3

DEDICATION

First and foremost I want to thank God for all he has done and continues to do in my life. Without him I am nothing. All that I have and all that is still to be accomplished will be because of him.

I would like to dedicate this book first to my wonderful wife, Sara, who encouraged me to follow my dreams and write this book. I thank you for your support—without you this book would simply be an unfulfilled dream and not a reality. I also want to dedicate this book to my three wonderful daughters: Taylor, Loryssa, and Torrie. Because of you I have learned how to accept and give love. I also thank my first wife, Michelle Lake. I am not the man I used to be, but you never judged me during those days when I was still dealing emotionally with my childhood trauma.

I also want to thank my two play mothers, Sharon Jones and Sandy Ballinger, for their encouragement. Michelle Buckman, you also have been instrumental in my life and have helped this book become a reality. I value our friendship. This book is also dedicated to my siblings, Richard, Joanna, Katrina, Dawn, and Cortez, my favorite aunt Thelma, her two daughters, Juliette and Dana, my cousins Esther, Cheryl, Anthony, and Merridia, and my aunt, Christine Butler. My confidant and best friend for close to forty years, Dr. David L. Taylor, and his wife, Maxine, have seen my struggles; you've seen my pain, my victories, and my healing. Not once in all of those years has your support, friendship, and love wavered. Thank you.

Last but not least, this book is dedicated to all the children who are dealing with childhood trauma even as I write this. This book is also dedicated to those adults who have yet to find healing and who are still dealing with the emotional and physical aspects of their childhood trauma. May you find comfort and peace is my prayer. Amen.

—Ira

TABLE OF CONTENTS

INTRODUCTION		ix
CASE STUDY 1	Grace	1
CASE STUDY 2	Russell	9
CASE STUDY 3	Esther	15
CASE STUDY 4	Abraham	23
CASE STUDY 5	Joanna	29
CASE STUDY 6	Jimmy	37
CASE STUDY 7	Jameson and Kathleen	45
CONCLUSION		53

INTRODUCTION

My education in childhood trauma began during my own childhood. My earliest memories of my parents are of waking in the middle of the night to the sound of their arguments. Verbal abuse was common and I witnessed many instances of physical abuse as well. While I was raised in a Christian home and attended Christian schools, I learned at an early age that there could be a vast divide between how the adults in my life taught me to behave and how they behaved themselves.

Eventually, my parents divorced. My father was awarded physical custody (which was unusual for the time), although both of them shared joint custody. My father worked two full-time jobs as a schoolteacher during the day and a postal worker at night. This meant that the usual routine during the week would be for our father to pick my siblings and me up from school and immediately drop us off with one of several babysitters. We would either spend the night at the babysitter's house or my father would come to pick us up when he was finished working at the post office (usually after two o'clock in the morning). On Fridays, he would drop us off at our mother's house to spend the weekend with her.

My mother had remarried shortly after the divorce and the home environment she provided could best be described as "toxic." Her disciplinary methods were simply abuse under the guise of parenting. These methods included being beaten with ironing cords, broom handles, sticks, cooking spoons, and an ice cream handle. The ice cream handle beating actually resulted in injuries that required several stitches in my head. If she thought I was lying, she would apply a hot knife to my tongue. I was paraded naked in front of my siblings while being forced to do menial chores. And, of course, there was constant verbal abuse.

There was little rhyme or reason to what would set my mother off, but the "punishments" certainly were not done for my benefit. She was not teaching my siblings or me right from wrong, nor discouraging bad behavior. She was simply torturing her children. Years later, when I confronted her on her abusive treatment, she tried pardoning her behavior by saying that she was abused as a child and that was simply the

Introduction

only way she knew how to raise children. Suffice it to say that I don't agree with the lesson my mother chose to learn from her own suffering. Years later, when I had children of my own, I learned a different method of parenting from the style of abuse and neglect that I was taught as a child.

For obvious reasons, I never felt safe, physically or emotionally, in my mother's presence. My youngest sister would often break into crying fits whenever my mother was around her (which obviously didn't improve my mother's mood and would often result in even more abusive treatment). Along with a father who was often physically absent, I learned from an early age to not rely on my parents for support (or, in my mother's case, even understanding). I absorbed myself in my studies, in sports, and in various church activities.

By the time I was sixteen, I realized that God was calling me to serve Him through pastoral ministry. At the time, I also had a strong desire to teach (specifically at a collegiate level), but it was not yet clear to me how I could do both things. The idea that a pastor could also be a teacher, indeed that a man could be more than one thing at the same time, did not occur to me. Years later, I learned that the conflicting drives to serve both God and one's fellow man is a struggle common to many people.

Of course, at the time I wasn't able to communicate these conflicting callings to my parents. In fact, my home life would grow far worse before it got better. When I was in tenth grade, the pattern of being raised by babysitters ended when my siblings and I went to live permanently with our mother. While the babysitters weren't a true substitute for time with our father, they were still preferable to the miserable conditions under which we lived on weekends; now there was no letting up in the constant cycle of abuse. I lived full time with my mother for a year until I finally moved back in with my father during my senior year of high school.

At the age of seventeen, I began attending Oakwood College. True to my calling, I studied Theology. I eventually earned a Bachelor's degree with a double major (Theology and Sociology) in 1981. But before I could become a minister, it would not be enough that I was called to serve; my calling would also have to be recognized by a religious organization. My father, for example, also studied theology, but his calling was never recognized by any institution. After graduation, I chose to serve the community as a social worker. But I wouldn't serve in the community where I'd been raised.

I left Chicago in 1982, shortly after graduation, and moved to Phoenix. My first job was counseling alcoholics at a halfway house. Later, I would work with senior citizens and actually helped to develop the first adult day program in Arizona. I spent a year counseling juvenile delinquents incarcerated for adult crimes, while at the same time running group therapy sessions for their parents. By counseling young and old, victims and perpetrators, I began to see how trauma could form a circle of abuse. I also saw the many forms that such abuse took and how the scars it left were often unseen.

Introduction

It was during my years in Phoenix that I also met my first wife. We met in church, shortly after I arrived in the city. At the time, I had few friends and no family in the area. Her family didn't care for me and actually forbade her from seeing me. I still don't know why they disliked me so much, but as is so often the case, their disapproval had exactly the opposite effect on our relationship. Eventually, we eloped. Even after our marriage, however, her family never truly accepted me.

My calling was finally recognized by the Seventh-Day Adventist Church in 1985. What followed was an 18-month internship before I could begin attending seminary. In 1986, my wife and I moved to Berrien Springs, Michigan, so I could attend the seminary there. At the time, I was still primarily following my calling to the ministry, despite all the things that I'd learned about myself during my years counseling in Phoenix. I had an empathetic ear for people suffering from childhood trauma, although at the time I still hadn't connected that empathy with my own childhood experiences. But I believed the call to serve God was greater than the desire to help my fellow man. It was during a graduate-level course in Pastoral Counseling that I finally realized that serving God and counseling those suffering from trauma need not be mutually exclusive. I could be both a minister and a counselor.

Before that Pastoral Counseling course, my only formal training in counseling had been a Psychology course I'd taken as an undergraduate. After that course, however, I began seeking out more opportunities to learn about the intricacies of counseling and empathetic listening.

I finished my seminary work in 1989, but it would take another two years before I was ordained as a minister. In the years following my ordination, I pastored at several churches of various sizes. No matter where I went, I would encounter couples and individuals whose problems could be traced back to childhood trauma. In 1995, I enrolled in a six-month Lay Counselor Training class/workshop at the Southern California Counseling Center. By the time I finished this workshop, I knew that this was the direction my ministry work was taking me. Until that point, I'd considered counseling to be simply a part (albeit an important part) of my overall ministry work. Now I realized that counseling would become the focus of my ministry.

Of course, it is often easier for us to see the problems and burdens of others than the ones we ourselves carry. While I was counseling other couples, my own marriage was slowly disintegrating. I had never properly addressed my own childhood traumas and instead learned to cope by keeping my wife emotionally distant. Ironically, by devoting so much of my time to counseling other couples and helping them grow more intimate and trusting, I was providing myself with an excuse to spend less time with my wife. How many times had I heard someone say that a husband or wife was really "married" to his or her job and never once seen a reflection of my own situation?

Introduction

I believe the Lord provides us with all the guidance we need if we only learn how to see His lessons all around us. How many times had I sat in rooms with men and women who described childhood abuse so similar to my experience? How many times did I see them grow up to enter unfulfilling relationships filled with emotional barriers, again so similar to my own? How many times did I give them advice and insight that, if only I heeded my own words, could have helped my wife and myself? In the end, I think it was pride that prevented me from seeing how much I had in common with those I was helping; I couldn't believe that a man with all my training and experience would ever fall into the same emotional traps as people who didn't know any better.

Eventually, I made the connection. I was counseling a couple who had grown emotionally distant due to childhood abuse. Both of them had suffered horrible abuses and had learned to build emotional walls very similar to the ones I'd built for myself. As I listened to their story, like so many stories I'd heard before, I finally realized that the empathy I was feeling wasn't simply a connection between a minister and a member of his ministry. It was one survivor of abuse seeing himself reflected in other survivors. Their story was my story. And the counseling I offered them could be offered back to myself.

Unfortunately, by the time I came to this realization, the damage done to my marriage was so great that it seemed past salvaging. Of course, it didn't help that I still wasn't willing to seek counseling for my problems. I acknowledged that my childhood trauma had caused me to become emotionally distant, after all. With all of the training I'd gone through, I didn't believe I'd need anyone else's help in overcoming my self-imposed barriers. Again, I blame my own pride for this failing.

But even as my marriage ended, I still had three amazing teachers present in my life who continued showing me that love and trust didn't always end in abuse. While my wife and I were always somewhat distant, my three daughters had never been conditioned to fear emotional vulnerability. I remember so many days of coming home after speaking with men and women who could not bear even to be touched, only to be overwhelmed by three girls racing to hug me. The love of children can be so pure, not compromised by agendas or suspicions, that adults often find it unbelievable. Before I had children, I'd always suspected that that sort of unconditional love was only the stuff of television shows.

I returned to my studies around the same time my marriage was ending. In 2002, I began working towards my Master's degree in Counseling. After earning my Master's degree, I knew that the next step would be a doctorate and in 2008, I enrolled in the Human Services PhD program (with a focus in Family Studies and Intervention Strategies) at Walden University. That same year, I received a Certificate in Clinical Ministry from Loma Linda Ministry. In 2010, I received another Certificate, this time in Clinical Mediation,

Introduction

again from Loma Linda. As of this writing, I'm currently working on my dissertation.

Which brings me to my reasons for writing this book.

The earliest lessons we learn are often the ones that we hold to be the most important, even when we see in later years that those early lessons were wrong (or at least misinterpreted). Those who suffer from childhood trauma often don't realize all the ways they sabotage their own happiness later in life; I didn't see it in myself and it was my job to point it out in others. When those closest to us (parents or other caregivers) become abusive, we learn to distrust anyone who claims to want what's best for us. When those closest to us abandon us, whether intentionally or not, we learn not to depend on anyone to always be there. When we are shown (or even directly told) that we are unworthy of love, we tend to believe it. And unless we learn to reach out for help, to swallow our pride and admit that we have been damaged by childhood trauma, it's likely that we'll end up teaching these same bad lessons to our own children.

Of course, it's easy to think of childhood trauma as something that happens to other people. When we hear about it on television or read about it, childhood trauma is always shown as something dramatic and obvious that leaves physical scars we can all see in graphic video footage or disturbing photographs. Childhood trauma is something that only evil people (whom we recognize as evil because they're always shown as disheveled and scowling in the coverage) do to obviously innocent people, without any word of justification. We're taught that there is no excuse for traumatizing a child and, while this is true, that doesn't mean that plenty of excuses aren't made. How many victims of abuse have been told that their treatment "wasn't that bad"? We can spend a lifetime excusing those who hurt us as not being as bad as the abusers we see on television, just as we can later excuse our own abusive behavior with the same comparisons.

In the chapters that follow, I will provide backgrounds on a number of individuals and couples whom I've counseled over the years. They are men and women from various backgrounds. The abuse they suffered ranges from verbal to emotional to physical to sexual. While I've tried to provide a cross-section of both backgrounds and types of abuse, I also want to stress how the coping mechanisms and long-term damage can be hauntingly similar. I will not be using their real names, both to give them anonymity and make them more relatable. These people could just as well be your friends or family members. They are not "other people." We are not "other people." You and I are not "other people."

It is my hope that someone reading this book recognizes some of his or her own pain in the stories. Acknowledging childhood trauma is the first step in better dealing with it. Of course, it is far from the final step and I encourage anyone who finds something familiar in these pages to seek counseling and not be too proud to accept help.

CASE STUDY 1

Grace

One of the saddest truths about surviving childhood trauma is that the skills we develop early in life to deal with abuse are actually quite effective at the time. It's only when we grow older and need to learn to deal with problems in different ways that returning to these tried and true methods becomes a problem.

"Grace" was the eldest of nine siblings. Her father was a church elder and she readily describes her home environment as a Christian home. However, her father was abusive, both physically and verbally, towards Grace, her mother, and her siblings. The abuse would include grabbing, punching, kicking, and name-calling. She notes that the abuse mainly occurred on the weekends and was sometimes fueled by alcohol. At one point, he struck Grace's mother so hard that she had to be hospitalized for two days and spent several weeks afterward in bed. Her father would likely not have considered himself to be abusive and was doubtless a very different person during the week when he was working (and sober).

In addition to being abusive, Grace's parents didn't bring in nearly enough money to properly raise so many children. She grew up in extreme poverty, typified by inadequate clothing and even malnutrition. Part of the problem centered on Grace's mother's constant willingness to forgive her husband and attempt to try again (without any real effort at addressing why the abusive behavior occurred). It was during many of these "forgive and forget" intervals that a new brother or sister would be conceived. With each new sibling, the family's financial situation grew more desperate and the resulting stress would grow more intense.

In some ways, Grace's father's relatively calm and mature behavior during the week would make the weekend outbursts that much worse. Grace saw enough of how a healthy family environment should function that she also understood that there was something very wrong with how her father behaved during his abusive periods. She was therefore embarrassed by the cycle of abuse and therefore more reluctant to report it to others.

Despite her embarrassment, Grace also took steps to end her father's abuse. Being the oldest of her siblings, she felt extremely protective of her brothers and sisters. This sense of protectiveness even extended over her mother, so that she would attempt to protect a grown woman when she herself was still a child. Grace would jump on her father's back and hit him with various objects when he grew abusive. She would attempt to physically shield her younger siblings from him. She even called her grandparents and asked for them to intervene.

Unfortunately, none of Grace's efforts changed the toxic environment in which she was raised. The abusive behavior didn't stop and no help was received from other people. When she was nineteen, Grace moved out of her parents' house to begin life on her own. She was married by the time she was twenty, which, unfortunately, did not give her the time or opportunity to properly deal with her childhood trauma. The strategies that helped her survive so long in an abusive environment would be the same strategies that made thriving in a healthy relationship all but impossible.

In order to survive emotionally, Grace had to keep herself detached from those around her, especially loved ones. Obviously, remaining emotionally distant and never fully trusting her husband led to marital trouble. The memories of physical abuse were still fresh in her mind and she'd learned that people could be rational most of the time, and then terribly abusive on rare occasions; since it was impossible to tell a potential abuser during his "calm" phase, she would simply suspect everyone of being a potential abuser.

Grace had also learned that there was no help to be gained from others, meaning she would have to take care of herself. She therefore felt an understandable need to control as much of her home environment as possible. Without understanding how abuse had shaped her outlook, her husband only saw a woman who was selfish, bossy, and unwilling to compromise on anything. He enjoyed dancing and going to movies, but she would routinely refuse to share in either activity. She would cite her religious beliefs as the reason for avoiding any sort of social activities, but in fact her refusal allowed her to remain at home (an environment more completely under her control). Her husband very quickly learned to live in two worlds, the fun and cooperative environment outside his home and the rigidly-controlled environment dominated by his wife.

A lack of spontaneity and need to constantly control those around her also led to difficulties in her sexual relationship with her husband. While Grace had never witnessed any sexual assault, it's not difficult to see how she developed a negative attitude towards sex. After one of her father's outbursts, her mother's forgiveness of him would often be accompanied by sex. Sex was a way of compromising with an abuser. And when her mother would invariably get pregnant, the resulting child would only further leave her dependent on her abusive husband.

Grace insisted on maintaining control of her body and emotions; thus she often refused her husband's sexual advances. Physical abuse had also left her ashamed of her body, so even when she did consent to sex, she could never fully relax and enjoy it. This lack of arousal would make sex painful for her, which only increased her reluctance.

Between Grace's reluctance to share any of her husband's outside interests, her need to control every element of their home environment, and her sexual unavailability, it's little surprise that her husband eventually began seeking emotional intimacy elsewhere. At first, Grace was oblivious to his affair. The only reason that her husband ever told her about it was that the woman with whom he was having the affair had threatened to tell Grace. Rather than having her find out that way, he chose to tell his wife himself.

While many couples cite infidelity for the reason a marriage ends, the fact is that there are many factors leading to an affair that make better reasons for ending a relationship. Simply put, an affair is often the symptom of a failed marriage rather than the cause. Even at this point, Grace and her husband could have used his confession as a starting point to rebuild their relationship.

Unfortunately, Grace's husband had his own shortcomings in dealing with relationship problems. He actually became physically abusive, punching her several times. Of course, physical abuse put the relationship back on familiar ground for Grace and she reacted the way she'd always reacted to such treatment: by fighting back. Soon, they were wrestling on the floor, exchanging blows just as her parents had done.

Unlike Grace's parents, however, Grace and her husband

separated after this altercation. They remained separated for a year, during which time Grace made no attempt to deal with her childhood trauma. Her husband had cheated on her, then physically attacked her, after all. She was clearly the wronged party and he was clearly "the bad guy." Forgiving him would simply be falling into the same trap her mother had fallen in time and again.

Despite the similarities to her own parents' relationship, Grace chose to reconcile with her husband. Unfortunately, what followed were five more years of similar behavior. Grace's husband had a number of affairs. He became more secretive around his wife and spent less time at home. Women would call their house, then hang up when Grace answered the phone. Their sexual relationship had also changed dramatically for the worse. Whereas they rarely had had sex early in the marriage, her husband began to simply force himself on her sexually, even when she refused. At one point, her husband even contracted chlamydia and passed it on to her. Eventually, they both agreed to a divorce.

When I first met Grace, she was 48 years old and had one daughter (who had no doubt witnessed a great deal of abuse between her parents, similar to how Grace herself had witnessed abuse during her childhood). That was over a year ago and (as of this writing) we still meet for counseling sessions, although not as frequently.

As with all my clients, I began our sessions by establishing a safe, empathetic, and sympathetic listening environment.

This was especially important with Grace, since she'd learned to approach every new situation as a hostile one, where she would have to fight for control. After two sessions, she began to feel comfortable enough to share what she was feeling.

In addition to our sessions, I encouraged her to begin journaling. Like many individuals suffering from childhood trauma, Grace would often re-experience past abuse whenever she recalled it. This is why it can be so difficult to get people to speak about this subject: We are in effect asking people to relive their physical, verbal, and sexual abuse every time we ask them to talk about it. In counseling circles, journaling is also called "putting it away," in effect stating the events in the past tense. In this way, Grace was able to develop some emotional distance between the abuse of her past and her present situation. Journaling helped her to understand, on an emotional level, that the verbal and physical abuse she suffered in childhood was no longer happening.

Grace would write out her journal at home and then read the entries during our sessions. By rereading the accounts, this helped to set up still another layer between the past and present. She was reading a written account of a past event instead of directly remembering it. In this way, she could look at her childhood self more objectively and better acknowledge the lessons that her younger self had learned.

Eventually, Grace began to see how she was sabotaging herself emotionally through her unwillingness to see other people's points of view or to compromise. While her father, mother, and ex-husband all behaved in terrible, often abusive, ways towards her, we were able to maintain the focus on Grace and what she could do for herself. After all, Grace was the only one seeking to change herself.

Eventually, I encouraged Grace to seek out and attend group therapy with other survivors of childhood trauma. When we first met, this would have been a terrible idea, since Grace would have likely treated the other members of a group as adversaries to be controlled (whether or not she realized she was doing it). For trauma survivors, group therapy should only be pursued once they feel safe around others. The two of us identified issues that she felt needed to be addressed in group therapy (getting mentally, socially, and physically healthy) and developed both long-term and short-term strategies for addressing them.

Grace needed to take the first step in learning to trust others by learning to trust me. Given my own background in dealing with childhood trauma, I understood how difficult it could be to trust and appreciated that she chose to trust me. It is my hope that group therapy will help her to develop trust in others.

CASE STUDY 2

Russell

"Russell" was the only child of a middle-class Christian couple. Starting at age seven, he recalls waking in the middle of the night to the sound of loud arguments between his parents. These arguments would often last for hours. Additionally, he witnessed repeated acts of physical abuse between his parents.

While Russell doesn't recall his father being abusive towards him, the same couldn't be said of his mother, who would often wait until his father left the house before taking out her aggression on her son. Besides being verbally abused and humiliated, Russell was also physically assaulted by his mother with slaps and kicks. Unlike many abusive households, however, his suffering wasn't confined to the home, as his mother would even visit him at school to humiliate him in front of his friends at lunchtime. She would yell at him in public, revealing embarrassing details about his life, as well as other family matters that he would have preferred to keep private. Furthermore, the meals she would pack for him would either have insufficient or inedible food.

When he asked his mother why she was so abusive towards him, her response would be that he reminded her of his father. In a strange way, Russell's mother was more self-aware than many abusive parents, in that she could verbalize a clear (albeit unfair and unreasonable) motive for expressing so much aggression towards her own son. While Russell's father was not directly involved in the abuse, his lack of action in protecting his son would teach him one of the terrible lessons that so many abuse survivors learn: No one will help you if you're being abused.

Like many such survivors, Russell eventually learned to keep to himself, preferring his own company to friendship or other relationships. The abuse continued until he was seventeen and went to college. While attending college, he didn't date much or form many friendships. While many colleges provide counseling services for students, it's only effective when those who need such services feel safe enough to seek them out. Despite the many opportunities he doubtless had for exploring healthier relationships, Russell had a relatively lonely college experience.

Eventually, Russell got married, but would continue to keep his feelings to himself, not even sharing them with his wife. The most effective method he used for staying emotionally distant from her was to simply maintain a physical distance between them. His job required long (often late) hours and he would frequently opt for overtime on top of that, thus providing him with an easy excuse for not being around. As I've stated already about my own background, being "married" to one's job is a tried-and-true method of avoiding intimacy. In addition to his job, he devoted a great deal of time to his hobbies, especially working in the garage (since he considered himself to be something of an amateur mechanic). When he did share time with his wife, he rarely spoke much and was often moody or temperamental. Obviously, sexual intimacy was also limited (almost nonexistent) between them.

Russell's hesitation to connect emotionally with his wife manifested in behavior very different than the treatment his mother inflicted on him. Starting with his second year of marriage, Russell began a string of affairs. His wife suspected these affairs were occurring and even confronted him about her suspicions on several occasions, but he was always able to convince her that he was remaining faithful. In fact, he wouldn't confess his infidelities until after their marriage ended.

Near the end of their marriage, Russell's wife tried to persuade him several times to seek counseling for his emotional distance. Even without knowing about the affairs, the marriage was clearly suffering (again, infidelity was a symptom rather than a cause of marital difficulty, and this time a symptom that only one of them even knew was occurring). Unfortunately, Russell was adamant that counseling wasn't needed and refused to seek therapy. Eventually, his wife filed for divorce and it's telling that Russell offered no resistance.

Russell and his wife had two sons together. It's curious (although not unprecedented) that neither Russell nor his wife have been abusive towards either of their sons. In fact, Russell's behavior might be better characterized as neglectful rather than overtly abusive, although neglect can leave its own brand of emotional scars as well. Hopefully, his sons have been spared the trauma that their father had to endure growing up.

Russell still didn't recognize that he had a problem after the end of his marriage. He didn't seek help until two years after his divorce. When I first met Russell, he was spiritually broken and taking a dim view towards life in general. As always, I began our sessions by working to establish trust and engender a sense of being in a safe environment.

Since Russell still had a great deal of trouble connecting his childhood trauma with the coping mechanisms that later destroyed his marriage, part of my work involved helping him to understand just how much damage had been inflicted on him. I encouraged Russell to try remaining emotionally present while verbalizing his memories of abuse. In some ways, it was the opposite of the treatment I suggested for Grace, since I felt Russell already had too much practice in distancing himself from his emotions. Of course, I made sure to continuously offer both support and empathy during his recollections.

Over time, Russell gained a sense of empowerment, finding his emotional voice. It is unfortunate that he didn't seek counseling sooner, before his marriage ended, but I am confident that he will be able to enter into future relationships with a greater emotional maturity.

CASE STUDY 3

Esther

"Esther" is a Latino woman whose parents divorced when she was very young. Shortly after the divorce, her mother completely abandoned Esther and her two older sisters, leaving her in the custody of her father. Unfortunately, her father became very depressed following the divorce and began drinking to excess. His drinking led to abusive behavior towards Esther and, when she no longer felt safe living with him, she moved in with one of her sisters. She was ten years old at the time.

Her sister lived in a two-bedroom house in another country. The community they lived in was a rural village that was very different from where she'd lived during the first ten years of her life. In fact, their house didn't even have indoor plumbing. By Esther's account, she was made to feel welcome. While her sister and brother-in-law shared one bedroom, Esther shared the other bedroom with her sister's two sons, aged four and six.

As Esther began to develop physically, however, she noticed that her brother-in-law was becoming more attracted to her. He would watch her whenever she was doing household chores (especially when she was wearing shorts or a skirt). If she was sitting down while wearing a skirt, he would often position himself so he could attempt to look up her dress. He also made a point of being nearby whenever she took a bath or had to use the outhouse.

But the nights were understandably the worst time for Esther. Her bedroom shared an adjoining door with her sister and brother-in-law's bedroom. He would slip into her bedroom and try to touch Esther almost every night. Most of the time, Esther was so afraid of her brother-in-law that she would pretend to be asleep, lying as still as possible until he actually reached her bed, at which point she would "wake up" and fight him off, causing him to flee back to his own bedroom. Curiously, this behavior seemed to have no effect on her brother-in-law's persistence.

At one point, Esther began locking the door between their bedrooms to make it more difficult for her brother-in-law to sneak in. However, he argued that the door needed to be left unlocked so that he could check on his sons at night. Like many victims of abuse, Esther blamed herself for what was happening and felt both guilt and shame, and so couldn't bring herself to explain to her sister exactly why she wanted to lock the door or what her brother-in-law was actually doing when he claimed to be checking on his sons.

Esther's next strategy was to position herself against the wall of the bedroom, placing her two younger nephews between herself and anyone entering the room. She reasoned that her brother-in-law would have to risk reaching over his two sleeping sons (and possibly waking them) if he wanted to touch her. She also began wearing tight-fitting clothes to sleep in, things that would be more difficult for him to casually lift up or pull down. Since he could find no rational argument against what part of the bed Esther slept on or what she wore to sleep in, this strategy was more effective than locking the door.

As I've mentioned earlier, the coping strategies that many survivors of abuse develop can be extremely effective in extreme situations. When presented with the problem of repelling a man's advances, Esther came up with the strategy of faking sleep and then attacking when he drew too close. When this strategy failed, she then began locking her bedroom door. When that strategy failed, she developed a third strategy, using her nephews as human shields against her brother-in-law. The fact that a ten-year-old girl could not only come up with multiple strategies but refuse to give up as each one failed, speaks to the resourcefulness and intelligence that many children display, even as they're enduring terrible trauma.

During the day, her brother-in-law would never bring up his nighttime visitations and conversations would run normally, as if nothing had happened. Esther's sister never suspected that he was doing anything wrong. Esther never told her.

Likewise, Esther never spoke to teachers or the authorities about the ongoing abuse, partially because of the shame and guilt she felt, but also because she understood that the laws in the country they were living in were quite different than laws in the United States. Sexual abuse and harassment towards women and children would often go unreported. If it was reported, the standard response by the authorities would be to sweep it under the rug. Of course, even in the United States, this was often the common practice (although improvements have been made in recent years), but Esther was living in a country where there were few legal remedies, even if her claims had been taken seriously. Furthermore, having been abandoned by her mother and unable to live with her father, she must have understood that there was nowhere else for her to go.

Eventually, her brother-in-law's unwanted attention wasn't limited to nighttime. Whenever Esther's sister had to leave the house during the day, she knew that he would try to touch her. To protect herself, Esther would often volunteer to watch her nephews when her sister was out, reasoning correctly that her brother-in-law wouldn't try anything with his sons present.

It's noteworthy that her brother-in-law probably had more to fear from his own sons discovering his behavior than the authorities.

This abusive environment lasted for five years, until Esther's father remarried and she went back to the United States to live with him. Once there, she eventually spoke with her other sister about what had happened. At the time, she pleaded with her sister not to tell anyone, especially not the sister she'd been living with when the abuse had occurred. However, her sister decided to share this information with the rest of the family. What followed was the outrage, shock, disbelief, anger, and blame that so often accompanies such revelations. The sister she'd lived with felt a great deal of guilt and remorse, blaming herself for what happened and her failure to notice the warning signs that both abuser and abused had worked so hard to conceal.

Esther is now 44 years old. She never married and has no children. Until recently, she was afraid and distrustful of men in general, preventing her from pursuing a lasting relationship. Her periods of depression and severe mood swings likewise made it difficult for her to form stable relationships. She also had a great deal of trouble relaxing at night, for obvious reasons, and would often suffer from bouts of insomnia. After years spent listening for every telltale sign of her brother-in-law's nighttime approach, it's not surprising to consider she would become hyper-vigilant to any normal sound heard while she was in bed.

Over time, Esther also suffered from both claustrophobia and agoraphobia. The claustrophobia is understandable, since most of the abuse she suffered was in the confined space of her bedroom; ironically, her inability to lock herself in a room made her afraid of closed spaces. At first glance, suffering from agoraphobia seems counterintuitive, since it's generally understood as being the opposite of claustrophobia. However, agoraphobia entails a great deal more than simply "fear of open spaces"; it's about fearing any unfamiliar environment, including public transportation, most workplaces, or even a therapist's office. Rather than considering claustrophobia and agoraphobia as two separate conditions, it might be easier to summarize that Esther had extreme difficulty feeling safe anywhere.

When Esther finally approached me eighteen months ago, she was feeling suicidal and was finally ready to confront the suffering that she was still going through due to abuse that had occurred three decades earlier. As always, my first goal was to establish a safe and trusting environment for her, a task made more difficult than usual by her agoraphobia. However, the burden she'd been living under had become so overwhelming that I didn't need to convince Esther of the need to deal with her childhood trauma.

As always, talking about childhood trauma is in many ways re-experiencing it. Together, Esther and I were able to put the abuse she'd suffered in a more mature context. She was now old enough to see that the abuse wasn't her fault. She could finally assign blame to her brother-in-law, as opposed to a fifteen-year-old girl living in a country where she had few rights (or to a sister who had no way of knowing what was happening).

Eventually, I directed Esther towards a support group, which provided her with an environment of individuals dealing with similar issues who could understand her situation and help her keep her past in the proper context. We are still meeting for regular counseling sessions at the time of this writing.

CASE STUDY 4

Abraham

Childhood trauma is in many ways a self-sustaining action that gets passed down, often unconsciously, from one generation to another. For this reason, the trauma suffered by "Abraham" has its roots in abuse suffered decades before he was even born. Both of his parents were abused as children themselves. Not only were they abused, but they also witnessed their parents (Abraham's grandparents) being physically and emotionally abusive towards each other. It would be a safe bet that Abraham's grandparents also suffered similar abuses in their respective childhoods. Not only does this cycle of witnessing abuse teach children a false narrative of how adults should behave, but it normalizes the behavior.

Since secrecy is a normal feature of such abuse, it also becomes easy to believe that such behavior is common, that "everyone does it."

As an only child, Abraham had no one with whom to share the abuse he suffered from both his parents. Since his parents were simply repeating the behavior of his grandparents, Abraham understood that he couldn't turn to them (nor, by extension, anyone else in his family). This abuse included name-calling, slapping, beatings (mostly administered by his mother when she was "in a bad mood"), and being deprived of affection or emotional attachment. At a young age, he was living in fear of his own parents, fear that he would do something that deserved punishment (with the assumption that physical abuse was a viable form of punishment). In addition to an ongoing sense of fear, Abraham also suffered from depression, a condition that would grow worse over time.

Abraham left home at the age of 22 and, shortly after, married his high school sweetheart. Like so many others who have suffered childhood trauma, the coping mechanisms he'd developed involved lying and denial. Throughout his marriage, he never told his wife about the abuse he'd suffered. She often suspected that he had suffered some form of abuse; besides the often vague emotional scars, there were plainly visible physical scars from some of the beatings he'd suffered. But he managed to explain the scars to her satisfaction.

It's likely that Abraham believed simply pretending the abuse had never happened was a viable means of moving past it. Later, he would tell me that he'd considered his marriage to be a fresh start for his life. Unfortunately, he'd never learned non-abusive methods of dealing with conflict and soon began to abuse his wife both physically and emotionally on a regular basis. It wasn't long before he realized that his own marriage was an almost perfect copy of his parents' marriage (and in turn their parents' marriages).

Abraham's wife filed for divorce shortly after they were married. Ironically, his wife (now ex-wife) only learned the extent of the abuse he'd suffered during their divorce proceedings. Had he been honest with her about the abuse and reached out for help, it's possible that he could have dealt with his own trauma, learned better methods of dealing with stress, and perhaps even salvaged their marriage. Since they had never had children, there was at least the reassurance that the cycle of abuse would end with him.

Unfortunately, Abraham was still suffering from the effects of childhood trauma, even without a wife or child to reenact the abuse he suffered. His fits of depression would often cause him to be late for work and withdraw from social situations. As he got older, these fits of depression grew longer and more intense. Tardiness gave way to a complete absence from his job for days at a time. The aloofness that had contributed to the end of his marriage also grew into near-total isolation. At first, he was able to make excuses for his tardiness and aloofness, but as his bouts grew more serious, his excuses couldn't keep up. His refusal to properly address his childhood trauma finally caused both his social and professional lives to completely fall apart.

Abraham did eventually realize that he had a serious problem that couldn't simply be ignored. Unfortunately, he was still unwilling to seek outside help. Believing that he could deal with his problems on his own, he tried to change himself through a series of self-help seminars and books. The shame and embarrassment he felt over his childhood abuse prevented him from sharing his problem with others, but that same shame and embarrassment also hindered any improvement he might have achieved through the various programs he tried. His attempts to change his thought patterns and life habits on his own yielded only brief results without any lasting effects.

At the same time, Abraham was trying to reach out socially, with equally brief results. He dated a series of different women over the years following his divorce, but would end each relationship before he became too emotionally attached.

Unable to improve his mood through self-help programs or short-term romantic relationships, Abraham eventually did reach out to someone else for help. His first choice was his doctor, who prescribed antidepressants. At the time, Abraham's depression had grown so intense that he was entertaining suicidal thoughts. While the medication served to alleviate some of the symptoms, it did little to address the underlying trauma that had caused his depression. While his moods grew less intensely dark, there was still the problem of needing the medication to maintain this state. Also, he had trouble remembering to take his medication regularly (which is a common issue for individuals taking antidepressants).

When Abraham finally came to me for counseling, he was suffering from feelings of not only depression, but also hopelessness. After all, he'd already tried ignoring the problem, self-help programs, and psychopharmaceuticals. Perhaps traditional therapy seemed like a backward step after trying the latest bestseller books and drug innovations. However, after only a month (as of this writing), we've already made impressive progress together.

As always, my first step was to establish a safe and empathetic environment for him to confront his trauma. The counseling process (as currently planned) will run in phases. We are currently going through the first phase of simply addressing Abraham's depression. As part of this phase, I've counseled him to continue his medical treatment (going back to the antidepressant medication his doctor had prescribed for him). At this point, we're also working to build up Abraham's self-image and find a support group and other resources that will help him reconnect with those around him. Once this phase is complete, the next phase will concern specifically addressing his childhood trauma. As always, it's important to remember that recalling childhood trauma can feel very much the same as reliving that trauma, so we need to wait until he is emotionally prepared for such an experience.

I'd like to stress that part of Abraham's counseling involves a return to his antidepressant medication. It is not my intention to suggest that traditional counseling is somehow better or mutually exclusive to psychopharmacology. By the same logic, a support group is not better, worse, or an alternative to one-on-one counseling or medication. Even the self-help books and seminars he tried were not without merit. These are all methods of reaching out for help and, when pursued in tandem, I believe they yield far greater results than when someone decides that any one method is the right way to heal.

CASE STUDY 5

Joanna

Childhood trauma occurs around the world, in families both rich and poor. "Joanna" grew up in Spain and from a young age was a witness to spousal abuse. Her father would regularly abuse her mother verbally and physically (although the abuse would be worse when he was intoxicated). The reason for this abuse was usually his suspicion that she was being unfaithful to him. Ironically, her father would frequently have affairs of his own, which were more or less open secrets.

Unfortunately, Joanna was raised in a culture where divorce was almost never an option (even in cases of infidelity or abuse), so her mother felt she wasn't able to leave her father. Of course, this culture would shape Joanna's own life choices, even after she left Spain to live in the United States, where the taboo against divorce is more or less nonexistent.

Joanna met "William" at a museum in Rome. William was an American investment banker on vacation. When he returned to the States, they began a long-distance relationship that culminated in marriage less than a year after their initial meeting. Perhaps understanding the mistakes they had made in their own marriage, Joanna's parents were opposed to their daughter getting married so quickly. They argued that she knew little about William or his family background. If they feared that William would become as abusive as Joanna's father, they never said as much, but the concern would have been valid.

In fact, within a month of getting married, William began verbally abusing Joanna. Within eight months, he began physically abusing her as well. As with Joanna's father, William's abuse stemmed from jealousy. He felt that Joanna brought too much attention to herself, encouraging men to flirt, stare, and make suggestive comments towards her. While Joanna was not actually seeking out such attention from strangers, she was a physically attractive woman who would just naturally draw at least some attention in public. William would often take this attention as being disrespectful towards him (not necessarily towards Joanna). Rather than showing his anger towards the men who flirted with his wife, he would wait until they were alone and then take out his aggression on her, blaming the actions of other men (and, in a way, himself) on her. The abuse began as simple yelling and name-calling. But it soon escalated into slapping, kicking, hair-pulling, and even punching. As always, it's interesting to note that, while William believed his abuse was justified, he was also aware that it was socially unacceptable (hence his waiting until they were alone).

The abuse grew so intense that eventually their neighbors began calling the police to intervene. Officers showed up at their home on two separate occasions for disturbing the peace calls. On both occasions, there were no outward signs that Joanna had been physically abused and so William was given a simple warning each time. It's telling that, even near the beginning of their relationship, Joanna was already maintaining the lies that perpetuated an abusive relationship, the same way her mother had never gone to the police or attempted to leave when Joanna was growing up. She maintained the illusion of normalcy despite the fact that they were living in the United States at this time, where accusations of abuse would likely have been taken more seriously.

Joanna and William had two children, "Markus" and "Taylor." On occasion, Markus (the older child) would place himself physically between his parents, demanding that his father stop verbally abusing his mother. Taylor would often hide under her bed when she heard her father begin to yell at her mother. In another curious parallel to Joanna's childhood, William was not physically abusive towards his children (although they had certainly witnessed his abuse of their mother), never doing more than raising his voice or threatening them with physical punishment.

It should also be noted that, while William and his two sons are all U.S. citizens, Joanna is classified as a permanent U.S. resident. Furthermore, as an investment banker, William earns approximately $170,000 a year, while Joanna only makes approximately $30,000 a year as an administrative assistant. When Joanna began considering divorce, it's impossible to say how much concerns over custody or even continued residency were on her mind. Between her husband's money, connections in the community, and citizenship, it would have been entirely rational for Joanna to believe that he might take full custody of her children. She might even have been at risk of being sent back to Spain, so that she wouldn't even be able to visit her children. While these scenarios were extremely unlikely, fear needn't be rational to be motivating. Coupled with the culture in which Joanna grew up, it's understandable that she stayed with William for as long as she did.

This situation continued for seven years, until the four of them took a vacation in Aruba. While in a restaurant, William became convinced that Joanna was flirting with one of the waiters. While he normally waited until they were alone before becoming abusive, this time William began screaming at his wife while they were still in the restaurant. He soon became physically violent and the authorities were called in to escort them both out of the restaurant. Once they were back at their hotel room, William began yelling at Joanna once again, but this time Joanna decided to yell back. Up until this point in their relationship, she had simply endured his abuse. Unfortunately, his response to her fresh defiance was to escalate the abuse from verbal to physical. When William began hitting his wife, the commotion woke up their children, who were sleeping in an adjoining room (and it's perhaps telling that they'd already grown so accustomed to verbal abuse that they could sleep through it).

William and Joanna had brought a nanny with them to Aruba to watch the children while they went sightseeing. When the nanny entered their hotel room to find the source of the commotion, she witnessed William hitting his wife. Since there was now an adult witness to the abuse, Joanna could no longer keep it a secret. Furthermore, she was beaten so badly on this occasion that she had to be taken to a hospital.

The authorities were contacted once again and, given the incident earlier in the restaurant and the fact that Joanna now had visible signs of physical abuse, they took the situation more seriously than the police had done on previous occasions. A social worker was called in to speak with Joanna while she was being treated for her injuries. Curiously, the social worker seemed more concerned about Joanna's ability to care for and protect her children than about Joanna's own safety. Joanna had remained silent for so long, in part out of fear of losing her children, and now her fears were being confirmed. She managed to convince the social worker that the physical abuse had been a one-time event and that a divorce was pending. She couldn't tell whether or not the social worker actually believed her, but she got the strong impression that she simply didn't want to press the issue.

Likewise, the Aruban government didn't take any drastic action against William. He was told to cut his vacation short and leave the country as soon as possible. Joanna and her children were allowed to stay until she recovered enough physically to make the trip back. Had this incident occurred in the United States, it's likely that William would have been arrested and the children turned over to Child Protective Services. However, given that they were tourists (and Joanna wasn't pressing charges), the Aruban government did little beyond physically separating William and Joanna for a brief time.

Once Joanna and her children were back in the United States, she filed for divorce. Despite her fears, she managed to retain custody of her children, as well as residence in their home. William moved into an apartment and (per court order) began paying both spousal and child support. The children reacted to this situation in different ways. Markus was willing to speak with his father, but was reluctant to actually see him. Taylor, on the other hand, was eager to see her father again and frequently asked if she could call him. Joanna had even overheard Taylor refer to her toys as "Daddy" when she was playing, although it should be noted that she would get visibly distressed and cover her ears whenever someone raised his or her voice in her presence. While Joanna recognized the need for her children to have their father in their lives, she was at a loss on how to re-integrate him into their family, since she couldn't imagine ever having a normal relationship with him.

It was at this point in Joanna's life that she sought help through counseling. Given the extent of the abuse she witnessed as a child and endured as an adult, the counseling process would take a great deal of time, first to establish the trust necessary for her to re-experience her childhood trauma, and then to confront how that trauma influenced her own behavior. Unfortunately, we only spent three months together before Joanna left the United States to visit her parents in Spain. She brought both children with her and has not returned to the United States. That was three years ago.

I have no idea if Joanna, her children, or her parents ever sought counseling in Spain, but hope that they all found a way to work through their respective experiences with abuse. I also don't know if William ever sought counseling, but Joanna had indicated that he apparently has no interest in pursuing a relationship with his children.

One of the unfortunate aspects of counseling is that, due to its voluntary nature, men and women sometimes stop before their recovery is finished. Sometimes people mistakenly believe that admitting a problem exists is the final step in the process (instead of merely the first). Sometimes they find the process so difficult emotionally that they decide to stop trying. Sometimes they simply grow impatient that counseling doesn't yield results quickly enough. Whatever the case, in these situations I am left not only with a frustration over not being able to help more, but also from not knowing how these life stories conclude.

CASE STUDY 6

Jimmy

Up to this point, I've focused on cases where childhood trauma was synonymous with abuse, either as a victim or a witness. However, severe trauma can still occur in the absence of abuse. "Jimmy" was born the youngest of eight siblings in south central Los Angeles. His father was arrested (for attempted armed robbery and assault with a deadly weapon) when Jimmy was only three years old. Due to his fifteen-year prison sentence (and the subsequent divorce from Jimmy's mother), Jimmy's father had little involvement in his life. Jimmy has only faint memories of his father before his arrest and has only visited him in prison a handful of times.

While both divorce and a prison sentence can lead to a

child feeling as if he or she has lost a parent, this is not really the source of Jimmy's trauma. With four brothers, three sisters, and his mother, he grew up in a family far larger than what the average child is raised in. Unfortunately, a larger family has only presented more chances for him to experience loss. His youngest sister (the sibling to whom he'd felt the strongest emotional connection) was killed in a drive-by shooting at the age of twelve. After her death, Jimmy became socially withdrawn. His other two sisters have pursued criminal activities and been in and out of jail for dealing drugs, assault, and theft. Three of his four brothers got involved with gang activity and were killed due to gang violence. His remaining brother is developmentally disabled, which led to him not getting involved in the criminal activities that removed so many other family members (either directly or indirectly) from Jimmy's life.

On one level, Jimmy could actually be considered a very fortunate young man. The household in which he grew up appears to predispose individuals to crime (given how five of his seven siblings turned to criminal activities). The one sister who did not become a criminal was killed before she was old enough to make such a choice. The one brother who did not become a criminal was physically incapable of doing so. It's actually rather remarkable that Jimmy chose a different way of life, despite the fact that he was physically capable of doing so and likely was presented with many of the same opportunities for it as his siblings.

Unfortunately, the constant cycle of losing family members to crime has taken a terrible emotional toll on Jimmy. Beginning with the death of his youngest sister, he became more isolated from other people, no doubt in an attempt to not suffer similar losses. As each brother or sister was killed or jailed, he would endure another childhood trauma (although each time less severe due to his withdrawal), while at the same time being offered yet another reason to continue withdrawing himself. He began suffering from regular bouts of depression and periods of inactivity. He also began having nightmares concerning violent deaths, to the point where he was unable to sleep.

It's worth noting again that neither Jimmy's mother nor his father (nor any of his older siblings) was physically or verbally abusive towards him. The trauma he suffered was the trauma of loss, which presents a different set of problems in coping. There is, for instance, no one to blame for such trauma. His family members did not leave him by choice, after all (although most of them could perhaps be blamed for the decisions they made that led to incarceration or death, with the exception of his youngest sister). When searching for a "bad guy" to blame, the culprit that presents itself is the world at large. Given how many of his family members have lost their lives or their freedom to various circumstances, it would be natural for a child to assume that the world in general is just a bad place, where no one is ever truly safe.

Not surprisingly, Jimmy devoted himself to his studies,

perhaps using it as an excuse to avoid interpersonal relationships as being "distractions." (This would be another example of the old habit of being married to one's work.) He earned a scholarship in engineering and was able to attend a local college. At the time, his mother had urged him to live on campus, but he opted to continue living with her, commuting daily to classes.

It's difficult to say why Jimmy's mother wanted her son to move out of the house. Perhaps she was already overwhelmed caring for his brother and didn't want to deal with another set of problems. Perhaps she felt the neighborhood they lived in was too dangerous and didn't want to risk losing another child to the criminal violence all around them. Or perhaps she simply recognized that her son was socially withdrawn to an unhealthy degree and wanted him to socialize more.

Academically, Jimmy did quite well in college, but he made few friends (and none of them close). He had trouble fitting in (no doubt due in part to his years of self-imposed isolation). He never pursued any romantic relationships, not due to lack of interest, but rather out of a fear of suffering another loss (either through rejection or some accident beyond anyone's control). Despite his excellent grades, Jimmy eventually dropped out of college, becoming even more reclusive. After dropping out, he spent most of his time in his bedroom, either reading or sleeping. He rarely interacted with anyone, including his family (and even then only after his mother would beg him to come out of his room and interact with them). Even when he was with his family, he would generally be very quiet, speaking only when directly questioned. He was unemployed and showed no interest in getting a job or doing anything else that would involve leaving the comfortable familiarity of his childhood home (specifically his bedroom).

I first came in contact with Jimmy two years ago, after he'd left college, when his former college guidance counselor recommended he try counseling. Given his reclusive nature, it was a challenge simply convincing him to leave the house and come see me. Getting him to discuss his feelings took a great deal of time and patience.

I should point out that individuals suffering loss-related trauma similar to Jimmy's can end up with a host of other problems that he's avoided. They can be extremely aggressive. They can develop substance-abuse problems. They can engage in high-risk sexual behaviors. Fortunately, Jimmy's behavior hadn't resulted in him getting into any physical danger.

I began our counseling sessions by focusing on grief and bereavement therapy. Jimmy had never found a healthy way to cope with his fear of abandonment, nor his sadness over losing so many family members. As I've written before, dealing with childhood trauma involves essentially reliving the experience. If anything, Jimmy's frequent nightmares were a way of reliving past trauma already; with counseling, he wasn't reliving that trauma alone.

When I felt he was ready, I referred Jimmy to a support group. For obvious reasons, connecting with a group of people (even people with similar problems) was going to be extremely difficult for him. While a support group is not a true family, there are enough similarities that the old fear of loss and abandonment would no doubt come into play. But so far, it seems that working in a group setting has helped him.

Jimmy's counseling also included assessment for Post Traumatic Stress Disorder (PTSD). For most people, PTSD is synonymous with military service, something from which only men and women who've been in combat zones suffer. But to a child, a community torn apart by gang violence would probably seem indistinguishable from a war zone, especially due to the fact that both gang members and non-gang members can be victims, just as soldiers and civilians are in danger during combat. As with many serving in the military, it's also possible that Jimmy could be suffering from survivor's guilt, unsure of why he's alive when so many members of his family are dead.

I've also been counseling Jimmy for his anxiety and depression, introducing spirituality (in the form of prayer and Bible study) to better ground him emotionally. When someone has lost so much (especially at a young age), it's understandable that he or she would view the world as an indifferent or even cruel place. Believing in a higher power that watches over us, even when we feel alone or threatened from all directions, can be more than a mere comfort; it can be a key to recovery. This synthesis of faith and therapy also provides me with reassurance that I was right to pursue my twin vocations of ministry and counseling.

CASE STUDY 7

Jameson and Kathleen

Whether it involves verbal, physical, or sexual abuse, one problem that continues to recur in situations of childhood trauma is the sense of powerlessness. A child is already vulnerable to so much in the world and the job of most parents is to keep him or her safe. All too often, the biggest problem parents face is that their children don't realize their own vulnerability, that they'll take unnecessary risks without understanding the accompanying danger. However, when dealing with trauma, the problem is often reversed. In those cases, children are all too aware of their vulnerability and view the world in general with fear. And this vulnerability is never made more apparent than when these children realize they can't even turn to their own parents for help.

"Jameson" and "Kathleen" are twins. They were raised in a wealthy household by two working parents. Their parents are both successful criminal defense attorneys who were not physically, verbally, or sexually abusive towards their children. Not only were all of their material needs met, but both Jameson and Kathleen had plenty of toys and other recreational items available to them as they were growing up.

Unfortunately, their parents' work schedules didn't allow them much time to spend with their children. They made sure that their children always had babysitters present until they turned four. Once they began attending school, there was a series of caregivers present, but never anyone whose presence was consistent enough to be seen as even a parental substitute. Jameson and Kathleen would regularly attend after-school programs, perhaps following their parents' examples of occupying themselves with activities that kept them away from home. By the time they were in high school, they were usually home alone until one or both of their parents returned from work.

In contrast, their parents were both raised in loving, supportive families that encouraged them to succeed. While they've both been successful in their careers, Kathleen and Jameson's parents have inadvertently failed to support their own children in the same way. As I've written earlier, neglect can be a form of abuse that's as damaging as any other.

Jameson and Kathleen were especially aware of this neglect when they spent time with friends and saw how they interacted with their parents. Again, abuse can become normalized, especially among children who've never known any other way of living, until they see how other people live. They would frequently speak with their parents about the differences in how their friends interacted with their parents, asking if they could spend more time with them. These conversations would normally end with their parents promising to be more engaged, but those promises would quickly be broken, thus reinforcing the idea that their parents could not be trusted.

Both Kathleen and Jameson did well in grade school. Unfortunately, they began to have problems once they began attending high school (although at first these were relatively minor). While they had an extremely strong relationship with one another, the neglect of their parents made them hesitant to form strong relationships with others. They learned to take care of themselves (and each other) from an early age, and while this can be seen as self-reliance, it can also lead to antisocial behavior. If not for their relationship with one another, it's easy to imagine either of them ending up with a more severe set of behavioral problems. As it is, beyond Jameson experimenting with marijuana as a teenager (hardly the most dangerous activity he could have become involved in), neither of them exhibited any severe behavioral problems… for a time.

Things changed when Kathleen was sexually assaulted at the age of sixteen by her boyfriend (and several of his friends). The assault happened at a party, where she was drugged without her knowledge. Unfortunately, it is estimated that between one in five and one in three women experience some form of sexual abuse before they reach adulthood. While horrifying, Kathleen's experience is all too common. Even with a supportive family and professional counseling, it can be difficult to work through the trauma.

Sadly, Kathleen did not have nearly the support network she needed to cope with what had happened. When she arrived home that night, she was visibly distraught and her brother immediately asked her what was wrong. When she told him, Jameson's first response was to blame himself, believing that he should have been at the party to protect his sister. This guilt drove him to seek out the young men who'd assaulted his sister and physically attack them. While guilt and anger are not necessarily the healthiest responses, Jameson at least demonstrated concern for his sister, as well as his assurance that what happened to her was both significant and not her fault.

Sadly, their parents' reaction was based more in fear than anger. Again, fear for their daughter's safety would have been understandable, but it became obvious that they were more concerned about how news of her sexual assault would affect them professionally. As criminal defense attorneys, they were concerned that having a daughter who'd been the victim of a criminal act might make potential clients think twice about working with them (especially if those potential clients were also accused of sexual assault). They advised their daughter to not report the event, essentially to pretend as if the whole thing had never happened. Being effective litigators, it's hardly surprising that they were able to convince a traumatized teenager to not report her own rape.

When I first met Kathleen and Jameson five years ago, Kathleen had begun withdrawing socially. She suffered from low self-esteem, panic attacks, depression, and anxiety. Jameson, on the other hand, was dealing with feelings of anger, guilt, and shame over his perceived role in his sister's attack. Initially, they attended counseling sessions together. Given the fact that Jameson was Kathleen's only source of emotional support, it made sense that he would be present during those early sessions, so that she would feel safe enough to relive her sexual assault when I asked her to describe the event. Likewise, Kathleen provided the needed support for Jameson when he opened up about his own feelings of responsibility.

Over time, I began counseling Jameson and Kathleen individually. While the trauma each suffered came from a different source (experiencing a sexual assault versus seeing a loved one trying to cope with being attacked), many of the behavioral problems the two of them were experiencing were decidedly similar. Feelings of powerlessness, fear that they would be blamed by others for what had happened, anger (towards Kathleen's attackers and their parents for not helping), and depression were common for both of them. Perhaps worst of all was the emotional numbing that both of them were beginning to evidence. When it becomes too difficult to process painful emotions (or, more specifically, when one simply doesn't know how to process such emotions), it becomes tempting to simply shut those emotions down. This, of course, can lead to long-term behavioral problems which the subject finds difficult to even acknowledge, much less work through.

After many attempts (several of which involved outright begging on my part), their parents finally agreed to participate in some of the counseling sessions as well. While Jameson and Kathleen had often characterized their parents as unfeeling (at least in regards to their children), it's worth noting that many parents feel uncomfortable attending counseling sessions with their children, even when they genuinely want them to get better. The sorts of things that get said in these sessions can be truths that the subjects have never admitted even to themselves, much less others.

Over time, our counseling sessions (both individually and as a group) yielded positive results. Jameson and Kathleen were able to put their traumatic experiences in a better context, so that they no longer blame themselves for what happened. Their parents have also developed better support skills. Both

Jameson and Kathleen (now adults) are still participating in support groups and experiencing a closer relationship with their parents.

CONCLUSION

Despite differences in race, gender, or economic status, there are far more similarities between survivors of childhood trauma. While I've always tried to approach each case as its own unique situation, over the years the similarities grow far too striking. Despite the greater media attention given to this subject, the image of a childhood trauma victim as being usually female and usually of a lower-class economic background is still pervasive. Likewise, the image of child abuse occurring at the hands of a male abuser, usually unemployed and/or uneducated, reinforces the idea in many survivors that what's happened to them can't really be abuse because abuse is something that happens to "other people."

What unites these survivors isn't a particular background or gender, but a particular worldview that they're forced to adopt in order to survive. The first lesson that every abuse victim is taught is that there is no help available. Grace's mother would constantly forgive her father and, as the eldest sibling, there were no older brothers or sisters she could turn to for help. Russell had no siblings and a father who made no effort to protect him from his abusive mother. Esther was abandoned by her mother and abused by her father, then found herself trapped in a country where even the authorities would not take her seriously. Abraham was raised by abusive parents who had themselves been raised by abusive parents, reinforcing the idea that his abuse was something that occurred in most families and that no one would sympathize with or help him. Joanna was raised in a country where divorce brought greater stigma than abuse and wives were simply expected to endure it. Jimmy had lost so much of his emotional support network to gang violence and incarceration that he couldn't trust anyone to stay long enough to help him. Jameson and Kathleen had heard so many broken promises from their parents that they eventually learned to trust no one but each other.

Another common factor that defines most childhood trauma is the notion that the survivors are somehow responsible for the abuse they've suffered, that they are the cause of it or at the very least could have prevented it. As the oldest child, Grace would take it upon herself to defend the rest of her family (including her mother) from her abusive father. Rather than asking for help, Esther implemented a series of strategies to make it more difficult for her brother-in-law to have physical access to her. Abraham came to believe that the abuse he suffered was simply punishment for his own bad behavior. Like her mother, Joanna was blamed for the attention she received from men, and taught that she was not only responsible for them flirting with her, but also for her husband's resulting jealous rages. Jameson directly blamed himself for the sexual abuse his sister suffered, simply because both of them had come to accept that no one else could be trusted.

Ironically, it is often the victims of childhood trauma who work hardest to protect the men and women who abuse them. Esther took various precautions against her brother-in-law's abuse, but never considered the most obvious solution of simply telling her sister what was happening. Abraham kept his abuse secret well into adulthood, not even telling his wife until after their marriage had ended. Even after being hospitalized, Joanna continued making excuses for her abusive husband, protecting him from the police on several occasions.

While some survivors of childhood trauma choose to remain alone as adults, many of them opt instead to get married at a young age, long before they've dealt with the emotional scars of their abuse. Grace, Russell, Abraham, and Joanna all got married before they'd dealt with their toxic coping mechanisms. Each of them ended up re-enacting the abusive relationships of their childhoods (either as victim or abuser), losing their spouses to divorce in the process. To be completely honest, I must admit that I also got married at a young age, before confronting how the abuse I'd suffered as a child had affected my own behavior.

While these survivors have something in common regarding their experiences and life decisions, the one thing that they all have in common when they first approached me for counseling was an unwillingness to form intimate relationships with others. Grace learned to view relationships in adversarial terms, with winners and losers, even treating her husband as a rival rather than a partner. Russell would lose himself in his work, his hobbies, and various sexual affairs, all while keeping his wife at an emotional distance. Esther never married and eventually developed agoraphobia, leaving her afraid to even physically leave her home, much less meet other people. Even when Abraham realized he had problems stemming from childhood trauma, he avoided reaching out to others, instead opting for self-help books, pharmaceuticals, and various other methods that wouldn't require him to make an emotional connection with another person. Joanna ceased her counseling sessions shortly after they began and (as far as I know) has still not worked through her childhood trauma. Jimmy refused to work, dropped out of school, had no friends, and rarely even left his bedroom. Jameson and Kathleen, while maintaining a strong relationship with one another, were unwilling to form strong emotional bonds with other people. Again, if I'm completely honest, I am also guilty of losing myself in my work rather than confronting the problems that childhood trauma caused in my own marriage.

Of course, while dwelling on the similarities, it's important to note the significant differences in how survivors cope. For instance, while it's common for survivors to mimic abusive relationships later in life, they can do so as either abusers or victims. Grace became obsessed with controlling her home and her marriage. Russell was not directly abusive, but rather neglectful towards his wife, not only through his obsession with work and hobbies, but also through a series of sexual affairs. Abraham became the abuser in his marriage. Joanna not only suffered the same abuse her mother suffered, but for more or less the same reasons (a husband's jealousy).

On the other hand, some survivors can be so traumatized that they simply refuse to pursue any sort of relationship (either romantic or platonic). Esther is now in her mid-forties, has never married, has never pursued a serious relationship, and rarely interacts with other people. Jameson and Kathleen are not involved in serious relationships (although both of them are still relatively young). Jimmy had become so isolated that he rarely left his bedroom. Even those who did pursue adult relationships (Grace, Russell, Abraham, and Joanna) would eventually divorce and withdraw, either by avoiding future relationships entirely or only pursuing relationships that were shallow (brief affairs and one-night stands).

Regardless of how they chose to cope with childhood trauma, the counseling process would always begin the same way. I would start by establishing a nonjudgmental environment where an individual could feel safe in recounting childhood trauma. As I've written, recounting childhood trauma can often feel identical to reliving the experience. For some people (such as Russell and Abraham), the challenge was maintaining an emotional connection during the recollection, so that the abuse would be understood as something more than just some events that happened in the distant past. For many others, of course, the emotional connection is clearly understood and the recollection needs to be done more dispassionately, with the detached understanding and perspective that comes with an adult mind.

Of course, whether recollection is accomplished to connect emotionally or observe dispassionately, the goal is to recognize how our past experiences influence our present behavior (and, once again, I have to make sure to include myself as someone who's gone through this process). As I've pointed out, children tend to develop coping mechanisms for the simple fact that, at the time, they work. Physically attacking an abusive father worked for Grace. Focusing on non-family activities worked for Russell. Being hyper-alert in bed worked for Esther. Frequent lying had worked for Abraham. Maintaining her abuser's silence had worked for Joanna. Refusing to grow emotionally attached to anyone had worked for

Jimmy. Choosing one person to trust and neglecting all others had worked for both Jameson and Kathleen.

In most of these cases, they could each cite circumstances when they'd veered away from these coping strategies and suffered for it. Esther revealing her abuse to one family member had nearly torn her family apart. Joanna speaking with a doctor about her injuries almost caused her to lose custody of her children. Kathleen choosing to date a young man who'd seemed trustworthy (and Jameson not trying to stop her from doing so) resulted in her sexual assault. Of course, the cause and effect of these situations is terribly misinterpreted (Esther's family wasn't truly torn apart, Joanna may not have been in any real danger of losing her children, neither Kathleen nor Jameson could have predicted what Kathleen's date was going to do), but the perception is reinforced. We often need very little evidence to reinforce the beliefs we already hold, no matter how clearly false they may seem to other people.

After establishing a safe place to discuss childhood trauma, recounting past events, connecting with those events emotionally, and putting them in a mature context, the next stage of counseling involves developing new approaches to relationships. Of course, there is again the double-edged sword of trust. On the one hand, I want to encourage people to open themselves up to potential new relationships and not to look at everyone around them as either potential abusers or potential victims. On the other hand, we all need to recognize that the potential for abuse exists and to be careful that we don't fall into familiar, destructive patterns of behavior. Basically, we learn to value and care for ourselves first, and then learn to value and care for others.

In addition to counseling, some of my clients also use Bible study, meditation, and medication to help them gain better focus regarding themselves and the world around them. Far from diminishing the importance of traditional counseling, these other methods can provide a necessary supplement to what I'm doing. There is, after all, no one-size-fits-all approach to emotional healing.

One resource that has been consistently effective for most of the individuals I've counseled has been a support group. For both men and women (who have often remained silent for decades about the abuse and neglect they suffered), speaking openly to a single person can feel like an act of courage, while speaking to a group feels simply impossible. It's rare that I recommend a support group during a first meeting, but teaching how to speak about one's experiences to a group of individuals is often one of my goals in counseling. Of course, the advantage of an abuse survivor speaking to a support group is that he or she will be speaking with people who have all gone through similar experiences. Not only does a good support group counteract the sense of isolation that so many trauma survivors endure, but it also shows that childhood trauma can affect people from all different backgrounds.

Finally, I help the individuals whom I've counseled to

accept that coping with trauma is an ongoing process. One of the problems that Abraham encountered during his various self-help ventures was the false notion that childhood trauma can be cured, that after a twelve-week or eight-step or five-stage program, the effects of childhood trauma can be erased and one no longer has to deal with them. Perhaps Joanna felt this way as well, ending our counseling sessions when she felt she was "over it." The fact is that, while the trauma remains, how we deal with it can change.

I wrote at the beginning of this book that I wanted to remove the sense of otherness from those suffering from childhood trauma. Many of the people who have come to me over the years feel this detachment from the general public, believing that their trauma makes them less able (or less worthy) of interacting with it. Many others go in the opposite direction, believing that, since they don't fit the preconceived notion of an abuse survivor, they're not really one of them.

Abuse can be sexual, physical, or verbal. It can happen to you if you're a boy or a girl, if your family is rich or poor, if your parents are pillars of the community or in prison. The childhood trauma that accompanies abuse affects more than the direct victims of it; if you simply witnessed a parent or sibling being abused, that in itself can be traumatic, especially if you somehow believe you could have stopped it from happening. Even neglect can, in its own way, be a form of abuse. You are not being selfish or melodramatic by seeking help.

When I began counseling survivors of childhood trauma,

I did so without consciously realizing my motivations. I would listen to stories that echoed my own every day, yet for years did not see the similarities. My inability to see my own coping mechanisms eventually cost me my own marriage. My own pride, that told me I was smart enough and emotionally strong enough to handle my own issues without needing any outside help, would have no doubt cost me any future relationships as well. Acknowledging that a problem exists is the traditional first step towards any solution. Reaching out for help is the next step. From there, it's a matter of sticking with the process, even when recalling abuse is emotionally difficult, even when acknowledging our own role in perpetuating cycles of abuse is shameful, even when we're just tired of talking about it and want to simply pretend the whole thing never happened.

The greatest gift I can take from my own experience is that it's given me the insight to help others. One of the goals of any support group, beyond helping ourselves, is to use what we've learned to help others in the group. Because after we learn that the world is a better place than we once believed, the next step is to help make it a better place than we once believed. I hope this book helps you on your way to that blessed goal.

CPSIA information can be obtained
at www.ICGtesting.com
Printed in the USA
LVHW081544130720
660544LV00035B/2657